The Manual: The Rules for Men

About The Manual

The Manual is a collection of tips for young men originally written in 2002. It uses strong language and includes adult themes. This updated edition deliberately seeks to remains true to the ethos of the original which was published under the *Jastoy* imprint.

Acknowledgments

My loving wife Oleander and my sons and daughter who inspire me, my sisters and brothers-in-law for sharing their collective wisdom, Sis Elayne who positively pushed me for this update, Sis Emma, Sis Oyin and all my friends who offered essential advice and support with this book when I needed it. And last but not least, the Creator and the Ancestors without whom, none of this would be possible. Ase.

About Ligali

Ligali is a Pan African Human Rights Organisation that challenges the misrepresentation of African people, culture and history in the British media.

The MANUAL

The Rules for Men

By

Toyin Agbetu

Under no circumstance are the contents of this book to be read by women

The Manual: The Rules for Men

Published by Ligali, Originally Published by Jastoy

Ligali
PO Box 1257, London, E5 OUD

Email: mail@ligali.org
Web: www.ligali.org
Tel: 020 8986 1984

ISBN 978-0-9543443-0-6

Second Edition: October 2011

A catalogue record for this book is available from the British Library

Disclaimer: Some of the images in this publication have been sourced in good faith from the public domain. They include public photos of models, actors, performers and the work of photographers and artists. I do not claim ownership of them and apologise if anyone is offended by their use. If there are any issues over their inclusion then please contact us and we will make the required amendment, either a credit or removal.

Dedicated to my father

In service to our family, with the spirit of our Ancestors

CONTENTS

THE INTRODUCTION

Greetings, congratulations on your purchase of this book for young men. By making this simple decision you have already taken a positive step towards enriching your life.

Now some things in *The Manual* are repeated more than once to hammer the point home. That's how we learn and trust me, you really need to remember this stuff and then put it into practice.

If all you want to know is how to get past her 'rules' then go to the back of this book. The answers are all there just before the section labelled 'the dark side', good luck. If you're still here with me, then good, you have patience, excellent. Following the instructions in this book requires self discipline, lots of it.

Now some of you may now be wondering what is *The Manual* really about? Well it's a brutally honest, tongue in cheek guide that's based on many of my own experiences, mistakes and in depth discussions with numerous male and female friends.

Please, don't take everything in it too seriously, if you want deep political and spiritual theory then go and check out one of my other books or films.

The Manual doesn't and can't include every topic, in every detail, but I hope you will find it provides a good starting point for stuff we need to know but don't know who to ask.

I am not and have never been a 'playa' so please don't read this if you're looking for tips on cheating. There also wasn't enough space to deal fully with the pain of breakups, heartache or loneliness. Instead it's my own humble attempt at fixing some of the dumb stuff us men do that maintains this 'singledom' gulf between the sexes and tips on how to deal with the strong physical urges and spiritual energy we as men have but don't always know how to control.

It's like some of the stuff your dad or uncle might have said after you've asked them an awkward question. Imagine a raw guide to help you through the minefield of relationships and emotions while giving some hints and tips on how to be a man.

I had wanted to include sections on running our own businesses, keeping out of trouble/prison, travelling the world, learning about self, fighting for self defence, cultural survival and succeeding at uni, but space did not permit so that will have to be in yet another edition.

Instead, consider this a self help text book for when you're at that time in life when you're growing up, need some independence from your parents, but the idea of meeting and successfully dating a woman seems more of a challenge than engaging with our traditional rites of passage!

Oh, and do not think *The Manual* will enable you to outsmart women, it won't. It will just give you an edge over those men that have not read it. The fact that you're reading this means somewhere else a woman is also reading this and developing counter measures for her fellow sistas.

If you try to use these tips to manipulate women then you will fail, always remember, they are smarter than us*.

Fact. Get over it.

By the way do not let her know that you've read this book, if she asks don't lie, just say... "You've seen it"

Toyin Agbetu

*Unless they are stuck on using 'The Rules'

Disclaimer: I'm not a doctor, I'm not a psychiatrist, I didn't rip anybody off and it's not based on anybody in real life, blah, blah, blah, ok...

First Contact

WHAT KIND OF GIRL DO I GO FOR?

The answer to this depends on you. If you're older than twenty then you shouldn't want a girl, you should be looking for a woman, but this depends on your maturity. If you're a 'club slut' then you're likely to attract good time 'party' girls. Someone who isn't serious about life, just wants to spend money, get drunk, have sex and move on when bored.

However, if you're no longer a boy and have grown up into a man, then you're likely to need a woman who is attractive, smart and loyal, a best friend fulfilling all your needs and desires of lover and companion, but in an honest, committed reciprocal relationship.

This Manual is designed to show you how to attract that woman who loves you and sees your potential as her man. A woman that will support and challenge you without making you feel small, a woman who you will one day see as being the one you choose to set up home and start a family with.

She exists and is waiting, but until you're ready, you will not find her and she will not see you, even if she's standing right in front of you.

WHERE DO I GO TO MEET A GOOD WOMAN?

There are good women all around you. The problem is that you will forever remain invisible to them unless you actively chose to do something positive with your life.

When we are working on a project that we enjoy, we tend to carry ourselves differently. We have passion, a buzz. Our mind is focused and has a clarity which translates into confidence and attractiveness.

It's like one of those martial art film messages, the true key to meeting a good woman is to not go out looking for one, but to work on something you are passionate about. You will recognise her when circumstances mean you both find each other.

WHY DO WOMEN REJECT ME AFTER FIRST CONTACT?

When most men are single they give of a 'hungry' signal that many women find unattractive. Likewise some women give of a 'desperate' vibe when they don't want to let a potential man that can provide happiness and security slip through their grasp.

She will dump you if it's obvious sex is the only thing on your mind, unless of course, you both want exactly the same thing as you have nothing else in common.

SHE'S PRETTY, BUT NOT MY TYPE, WHY CAN'T I STOP THINKING ABOUT HER?

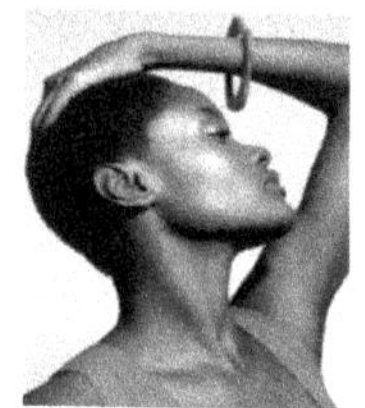

Contrary to some of the foolishness peddled out on TV and films, the best relationships are made between people who share vision and purpose, not just physical attraction. What this means is that we often fall for women, at, or on the way to places where we work or chill.

All of us are physical and spiritual beings. As such if you meet someone who you feel comfortable and compatible with on both these levels, then Mother Nature will help you realise that she is your 'type'.

HOW DO I STOP MYSELF FROM DROOLING LIKE AN IDIOT?

- It is imperative you understand that no matter how sexy she looks she's NOT just sex on legs, she's a woman with a ruthlessly efficient brain.
- If she has long legs to heaven then remind yourself that the entrance is through her mind, not skirt.
- If you meet a large breasted woman you MUST do these two things...

  1. Ask yourself what colour eyes does she have?

  2. Play blink, best of five.

GAL (18-21) - She's trying to find herself, interested in sexploration. Potentially very fickle. Any idea of a serious long term relationship is clutching at straws.

This is the time when many engage in fun and exploration. Enjoy yourself but be responsible.

YOUNG WOMAN (21-27) - The wonder years. She's more confident, has a better sense of who she wants to be, and where she'd like to go although she's not 100% sure yet. She's now also beginning to have a strong idea of what she doesn't like, which in turn helps her develop character.

This is the time to start getting serious, anyone who is still obsessing about parties and nightclubs will just get you into trouble.

WOMAN (28-35+) - The holy grail. She's ready for commitment, but still wants to have fun, she may be interested in children and a family, but she still wants to live life first. If you can handle a woman who's no longer easy to manipulate because she now has control of her insecurities then this is the one.

Oh and she's at her sexual peak.

HOW DO I INTRODUCE MYSELF?

- Make sure you're presentable; be casual in attitude, but not over familiar. Smile. Work to make the first encounter brief but memorable. Not long and forgettable!

- Approach her confidently, if you're wearing shades then take them off and give her eye contact. Next, ditch any corny chat up lines, and simply say hello with a smile.

- Ask her name, and remember to use it.

- Look at what she's wearing, LISTEN to what she's saying, is there anything unique about her? Something you both have in common? Explore it with her.

- Use (but don't abuse) eye contact, a lot of initial flirting is done without any spoken words. But don't stare at her like a potential psychopathic stalker.

- Be confident, not arrogant, don't fidget, remember shy guys come last.

- Ask her an original question that can't be responded with a yes/no answer.

- If using flattery avoid clichés, when using flattery. Compliment her appearance without stating the obvious. i.e. "you have nice big breasts" could be "you look great in that top".

- Always remember many attractive people are used to everybody telling them they are good looking, instead compliment her on something she's done or achieved.

- Be honest about who you are and what you do. Don't brag, it's an unattractive trait.

- If you can't dance then don't until you learn. No one really wants to be associated with, or trodden on by someone who doesn't realise they've got two left feet.

- Initiate subtle physical contact (i.e. find a valid reason to briefly touch or hold her hand - but NOT her face).

- Remember all that glitters is not gold, the quiet girl sitting in the corner observing everyone else is possible the most dynamic person in the room.

Women with too much makeup on are often carrying more than excess chemicals on their face. Some are (unsuccessfully) trying to hide their insecurities over how they look.

If their face looks like a mask then be careful of the cracks that can appear as the foundation melts away. The best look for a woman is when she's so natural (and at peace with herself) that you don't even notice she has makeup on (other than around her lips and eyes).

- Find a reason to whisper to her, it brings you close enough to smell one another. Don't do this if you're sweating (i.e. stinking like a pig).

- Feistyness - Being cheeky and being rude is not the same thing. Watch how she is with strangers to get an idea how she could be with you.

WHAT DO I TALK ABOUT?

Do's

Try and make sure she talks more than 70% of the conversation. Use the "why?" technique to keep her talking about herself. Look for shared areas of interest and add to the conversation. You'll have your chance later on if it goes well.

A woman wants to know how you see her, if she thinks you could one day be serious about her, then she'll consider thinking seriously about you.

If you have children don't hide it, tell her, show her the pictures in your wallet, BUT make sure a picture of their mother is not inside.

If she has children try and always remember their names

Although they are time wasters, don't totally knock TV soaps especially if you're into sports (be clever, learn the basic plot lines from a TV guide and join in). Try encouraging her to watch some more interesting dramas as well. Beware women who think ruthlessness without compassion is an attractive trait.

Remember most women are the absolute emotional opposite of men, hence achieving spiritual chemistry will ultimately create physical chemistry.

Don'ts

Don't exaggerate trying to impress. She'll be curious about you and want to share details of your meeting with her friends. Don't give any of her jealous friend's reason to tell her to dump you.

If when talking to a woman for the first time the topic of what car you drive enters the conversation then give it up, the relationship will fail.

Don't talk sport. Be interesting instead.

Don't try to talk about a topic you have no knowledge on. If she susses it out then you just look a total loser.

Don't tease her by offering more than you're prepared to give (e.g. marriage!).

Don't just talk about her body, it may be fun for you, but it's likely to be a turn off for her if she thinks you're only interested in sex.

HOW DO I KNOW IF SHE'S INTERESTED

Good signs

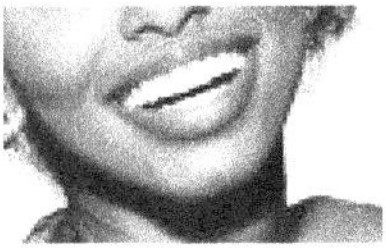

- She's smiling and listening to every word you say.
- She leaves her friends to talk exclusively with you.
- She flicks/plays with her hair or licks her lips (this is often a subconscious action so don't make assumptions).

Bad signs

- She's avoiding eye contact with you.
- Silence. Most women hate silence, if she isn't talking then be afraid.
- She uses the 'I've just remembered I've got to call someone' line.
- She keeps looking at her watch or text messaging.
- She uses the 'I've got to visit the girls room, maybe we will meet up later' line.

HOW DO I GET HER NUMBER

Mention being interested in knowing more about her at a later date, if you're doing very well then she may just give it without you asking.

If she's talking more work than play then pay good attention to what she does for a living and look for a valid reason to ask for a business card.

You (and colleagues) or her are making moves to leave, give her your number (preferably on a plain business card, write your home/mobile number on the back in front of her) and say "Hey, I really enjoyed talking to you (take out pen & find a scrap of paper or better yet another business card), give me a number so I can contact you again".

A. Sincere Brother
123 A Good, Clean Space, Somewhere AFR07

t: 020 7123 4567
e: a.sincere@imseriousaboutwhatido.com
w: www.imseriousaboutwhatido.com

Failing that...

... just ask her.

Don't be vulgar

Always use 'please', 'thank you' and 'excuse me' in formal conversation. This is especially when someone else is being rude. If you can't discipline your own mouth, then you won't have it over your actions.

Keep your cool especially when everyone around you is losing theirs.

Learn to control your temper. You do not need to raise your voice when others are losing their mind. Listen, observe and stay in control. By staying cool calm and collected you are in the perfect position to swiftly take control of the situation once the initial heat burns out. Wait and then strike, quietly and deadly.

Do not boast about money in public.

Your finances are your personal business. Unless there is a specific reason to share financial details with a room (i.e. fundraising) then don't do it.

Be courteous to everyone.

Never look down at anyone in a room and treat everyone with basic respect. This applies to the CEO, cleaners, cooks and security guards.

Don't be late for a meeting.

Always arrive at least 15 minutes before the agreed time. If you are late then the first thing to come out of your mouth should be an apology, not an excuse.

Don't be stupid

If you don't understand what is being said either ask for clarity or shut up

Listen but never gossip

Don't tell everyone all your business and likewise don't share the private details of people you know. It shows you can be untrustworthy.

If you make a promise, keep it.

As a man, there is little of greater value than your integrity. If you say you're going to do something, do it. If you can't, then admit it. If you can't be trusted on your word, then you won't be trusted period.

Be assertive when required.

If you're too polite you come across as 'nice' & spineless.

The Call

DON'T call after a few hours it's oh so desperate. Have patience. Give her a little time to think about the time you spent and miss you. If you really can't wait, then send a text to thank her for making your evening enjoyable, nothing more or you will mess it up.

If you liked her then call her the next day, early evening. If she's answering thank her for a great evening, if she's not, then leave a message (she has caller id) and ask her to ring you back. Make sure the message is no more than 30 seconds.

Don't ask her out more than once.

When you call her, avoid the topic of sex unless she initiates it, the objective here is to learn who she is.

Do NOT tell her you love her, you don't even know her yet you plum!

Do not send naked pictures of yourself to her mobile.

TIMES 2 CALL

8:00 - 10:00 am	Don't be silly, she's getting ready for the day
11:00 - 4:00 pm	By appointment only, she uses this time to do her stuff
5:00 - 7:00 pm	Risky business, she's getting ready to be herself after a tough day.
8:00 - 10:00 pm	The magic period, she's eaten, relaxed, and wants to chat (make sure you don't clash with her favourite TV program)
11:00 - 12:00 pm	The danger hour, if she likes you then she'll be feeling tired, but hopefully sexy, if you're just a friend then she'll be tired and possibly annoyed

Listen, listen and listen - ask her a question, STFU and listen to her response without interrupting. Don't worry your time to talk will come.

Describe what she was wearing the first time you met, compliment her choice.

Explain what attracted you to her only using her physical attributes as backup.

Never slag off an ex, it was also your fault that your last relationship failed, let her decide who was really to blame.

Invite her to dinner at a mutually central location. If you're planning on going to a restaurant then remember to check if she's vegetarian and have two locations in mind before starting the conversation.

Don't lie to her. Women instinctively store minute details from all previous conversations you have with them, enabling them to detect a lie with incredible accuracy. Honesty is the best policy.

Make a decision and tell her what you'd like to do next, ask her opinion and if you both disagree try and meet in the middle.

If she doesn't know the venue and asks, tell her to either dress casual or dress to impress (note: women love to dress to impress).

If you drive, then offer to pick her up, but not from her home unless she has already given you the address.

If she's introduced sex into your discussions and is comfortable with you reciprocating, then remember to randomly send her short sexy messages, no explicit words leave everything to the imagination, remember... less is more.

A man who lives with his parents is not seen as sexy, if that's you then arrange to meet outside.

Set yourself a call time limit of a couple of hours, try to deliberately finish the conversation leaving both of you wanting to talk more...

If you don't want to go for a dinner date try a comedy club. Laughter is always good to get you both smiling.

Do not take her to the cinema on the first date, you don't get to speak during the film and unless it's a scary movie there is little space for contact.

Try to talk half as much as you listen, when nervous we either clam up or babble too much. This can happen in scenarios where there is silence and nobody is stepping up to the plate. If you must say something ask a question.

DATE IDEAS

- Picnic in the park
- Music or theatrical event at a small local venue
- Drive to the coast and catch sunset
- A Museum or Gallery
- Bookshop or Creative reading / writing session
- Local Café (daytime) / Restaurant (evening)
- Spoken Word / Poetry Event
- Comedy Club
- Wine bars

The Date

Most women are looking for 'the one' to complete her (sometimes even within their current relationship), convincing her that you believe she is your Miss Right, is a vital step to stop her looking any further, the date is an indication that you've passed the pre interview, this is now the REAL test.

WHAT ARE SOME OF THE MISTAKES THAT I SHOULD WATCH OUT FOR WHILE GETTING READY?

Make sure you have enough cash in your wallet, even if you intend to pay for everything on a card.

Brush your teeth, cut or clean your finger nails.

Make sure you have fresh breath, chew gum, suck mints, but avoid garlic or cheese and onion crisps!

When using cologne, remember her sense of smell is greater than yours, if it smells strong to you, then it's gonna be overkill for her.

Don't take an mp3 player or pocket video game machine with you on the date. It's not only boring, but also rude. If you really want to impress, take a book.

Do not wear any novelty items (ties, t-shirts, etc). Today is about making a good impression and people judge us by what we wear. If this bothers you then you should choose to wear what you want people to think.

Aim to look neat and clean, it is always better to be a little overdressed than under. You don't need a tie but a jacket would be nice. No suit though and definitely no t-shirts with 'funny' messages. Many women are also obsessed with shoes, if you're a trainer person than wear the plainest black pair you have (as a man you should own two pairs of trainer's maximum).

Don't judge her by her clothes. Just because she looks sexy doesn't mean she wants sex with you. Listen to her words, act accordingly.

No flowers, but a small gift like chocolate is cool

Print a map or plan the route in advance

WARNING: Good women are not impressed by designer clothes, if she knows the exact price of your shirt or shoes on sight, then she's probably working up to learning the pin on your gold credit card, which you could ultimately give to her!

SHE LOOKS GREAT! HOW DO I NOT F*CK THIS UP (DINNER DATES)

DONT be late, put it in your diary, phone or electronic organiser 30 min earlier, sleep outside the restaurant if need be, but NEVER be late. She on the other hand can be up to an hour late, any later without a call to apologise is enough reason to go home and forget she ever existed.

If it's obvious she's made an effort to look good then compliment her. In fact, just by virtue that's she's going out with YOU deserves a compliment. Tell her "You look great/good/nice (or 'well' if you truly don't like what she's wearing)".

Remember she's a woman, she wants to be treated differently but with equality, there's a thin line between chivalry & chauvinism.

If the road is busy & crowded then reach to hold her hand while crossing it.

Beware a woman whose phone is colour coordinated with her clothes AND nails, she's way too picky for you.

Always pay for her drinks, say no if she offers to buy you one - BUT if she insists, smile and accept.

If your phone rings then apologise, answer it in front of her, then turn it off or if you're expecting an urgent call put it on silent, vibrate or activate voicemail.

When selecting from the menu, don't be afraid to be decisive and order different food. It gives you an opportunity to offer her some from your plate later on to let her see how it tastes.

When entering a restaurant together, open the door for her and wait till she's seated before sitting down. Don't eat until you both have food, or have shared your starters

Women hate a man who is overly possessive (insecurity), but feel valued & treasured when they know you are a little jealous of another man.

Never take her to a fast food joint while dating. If you must do cheap, do it with style and go for a romantic park picnic.

No burping, farts and close your mouth when chewing.

Most women are turned on by men who display confidence, compassion, sincerity, and honesty.

Ask her questions, moral dilemmas are best, women love to talk, and you learn a lot about who she is.

CHIVALRY TIPS

She's important

If you're outside at a public venue and she enters the room to meet you, stand up as she approaches.

Hold the door open

It may seem old fashioned but showing courtesy in this manner helps makes her feel welcome.

Offer her your jacket if it's cold

She often wears clothes that look great but are impractical, she did it to impress you. If it's cold and she's shivering, man up and wrap her inside your jacket, she may even ask you to join her to share body heat.

Never place her call on hold

If a phone call is that important ask her if you can call her back. In fact disable call waiting its rude and designed to make the phone company money

If you don't want her to think of you as tight then tip good service at restaurants. Don't be flash with it (a subtle 10% is good enough).

Intelligence and humour are great aphrodisiacs. Many women love to flirt and adore a man who can flirt back, just don't forget to romance her in between. DON'T rush it.

Whilst some women love a good debate, too much sarcasm is not charming. Don't be afraid to disagree but know when to back down and listen without getting in her face.

If the date is in the daytime, take it easy, it's a prelude.

Good signs

- After your date she calls you to tell you she thinks she lost her 'earring' in your car.

- She gives you an "I forgot to ask you..." call

Bad signs

- She tells you about a guy she fancies.

- She's constantly updating her Facebook and Twitter pages whilst she's with you.

DINNER WENT PERFECT NOW HOW DO I GET TO TAKE HER HOME?

- It should be quite late, make sure you haven't had too much to drink, insist that you're not letting her travel home alone...

- If you drive then offer to drop her home but ask if it's ok to detour by your home first to get something (a gift) for her. She'll ask what, tell her it's a surprise and leave her guessing.

- Drive or take a cab home and give her the gift (if you have no ideas then try a single rose or hand written card). She may find it corny but will appreciate the romantic thought.

- Drop her home and then kiss her on the cheek, hold back from more to show you respect her. First date sex is almost always a recipe for a disastrous relationship.

- If she wants to stay at yours then sleep on the sofa with her, do not attempt to trouble her (especially if she is not sober). If things are going well you can ask her if she wants a massage but if she says no then it means no.

- If she has special dietary needs TAKE NOTE and buy them BEFORE she comes round (e.g. no dairy then soya milk, vegetarian then no meat etc).

STUFF YOU SHOULD HAVE ON DISPLAY IF SHE'S COMING ROUND TO VISIT FOR THE FIRST TIME

It goes without saying your place MUST be clean, tidy and smell fresh, if you want to increase the chances of her staying over then...

LOUNGE

- Pictures of mum, dad and any children you may have.
- A plant.
- Books (not for show, you must have read some)
- Soft lights (either dimmers, lamps or uplighters)

BEDROOM

- Clean sheets on bed and a plain quilt/duvet WITHOUT nerdy cartoon pictures on it.
- At least two pillows
- A bottle of olive or almond oil (failing that Vaseline or baby oil)
- Tissues.

BATHROOM

- Two bath towels & one hand towel.
- One toothbrush (plus packet of spares)
- Liquid hand wash / Shower gel / Soap

KITCHEN

- Food in fridge (some women use this as a barometer to your current financial status).
- Fresh fruit (this indicates a healthy attitude)

- No tooth to tooth contact.
- Use your finger to feel her neck and cheeks during.
- Vary the intensity from soft, to strong, from firm to gentle.
- Intensify that key moment, tease her gently by starting with a gentle kiss on her neck, then between the eyes, then the nose, then when it's right... the lips.
- A little tongue, not too often...
- Occasionally inhale and take her breath away...
- Use your hand to hold her firmly, exploring her back, butt and resting on her hips.
- Close your eyes and feel the magic

Sex Tips

Once you've had sex with her you can NEVER be just 'friends', make it worthwhile by memorising these tips.

HOW 2 PLEASE HER SEXUALLY

Most women need to be romanced before she is turned on for sex... and by romanced I don't mean saying "I love you lets f*ck!" The secret to seduction is understanding how to read her mood & create that perfect balance of vibe & passion.

Good music, some food, soft lights, naturally flowing two way conversation and being tactile without coming across as a leach will always bring rewards. Remember foreplay begins fully dressed.

If the mood is right, ask her to dance and hold her close.

Kiss her, start on the lips and move... everywhere (don't slurp and make sure you brushed your teeth thoroughly that day). Kiss her cheek, her neck, hold her close, rest your hands on her hips, support her back and return to her lips.

- Tease her, take your time during foreplay.
- Let her guide and then take the lead.
- Slow down.

Remember, a woman CAN enjoy sex without having an orgasm, but don't make a habit of it.

If you have a serious problem with popping too early then 'practice' prior to the task at hand.

WARNING - Size does matter, any woman who has told you otherwise either loves you or is cheating on you.

If you are not well endowed it's not the end of the world. Luckily for you women's bodies are far more sensitive than men's. The solution is to score ten out of ten on her other zones.

Oral stimulation IS foreplay, she still wants the main course, even if she came.

If you masturbate then don't do it for at least three days before now, that way you can be sure of being at peak performance.

Any woman prepared to give head while she is 'on' is incredible - NEVER, EVER cheat on her.

Do's (PRE)

- Slow and intense is the key, kiss her, talk to her while undressing her.
- Try giving her a foot massage.
- Try playing with her hair or gently stroking the back of her head, while kissing.
- Never ignore her breasts, be gentle they may be sensitive.
- Learn the one handed bra removal technique – this is achieved by squeezing the back of the bra together making it far easier to unclip. Remember not all bra's fasten from the back though. 
- Learn the (hand to feet) panty removal technique – this is achieved using the hand as a shoe horn around her butt approach.
- Give her a full body mouth massage (i.e. kiss her all over).
- STD's and HIV are real, so are babies - use protection because the withdrawal method is not 100% reliable.
- As long as you respect her dignity - anywhere, anytime, even in (private) public spaces.

During

- Remember to look into her eyes.
- Talk to her, some women love dirty talk, some enjoy funny talk, so try and see if it arouses her.
- Say her name, let her know it's her you're making love to and not some fantasy woman in your head.
- Kissing, lots of it.
- The average duration is 15 minutes, she wants a MINIMUM of half an hour, do this right and she'll be boasting to her friends.

- If you must fantasise about other women then use them as a supporting 'cast' for her. She MUST be your number one.
- Alter speed of thrust and direction of motion

After

- Hand her some tissues.
- Hold her, kiss her, talk to her, try and stay awake, at least for a little while, have a sweet drink or fruit if necessary (for energy).

- Sleep with her head on your chest or lie in the 'spoon' position with her.
- A lot of women love early morning wakeup sex, but to do it correctly she must wake up to feel you caressing & loving her, NOT just inside her, she may feel violated.

Don'ts

- Don't clock watch
- Don't ask comparison questions (about her previous lovers)
- Don't try to enter if she's tense and not wet enough.
- Don't keep asking her if she came... if you don't know, then you never will and besides... it just pisses her off. (NOTE: When she comes her vagina will make tiny contractions. Depending on your 'fit' you should be able to feel this).
- NEVER do anal. NEVER... EVER.
- Try not to walk with condoms in your wallet, but if you really cannot restrain yourself if the moment arises then leave a packet hidden in a discreet place, e.g. a car glove box.
- Don't sleep in the wet patch... that's her duty

HOW CAN I MAKE SURE SHE COMES

By remembering the 'ladies first' rule... always try to make sure she comes first... trust me you won't be long after.

Many women don't achieve orgasm through penetration OR oral sex. Direct clitoral stimulation using your tongue (or finger love) may be the only way to save the day, think of her clitoris as the equivalent of a female penis. Remember, ask what turns her on. It reveals consideration as a lover, she may then ask you!

> **Always remember that the most sensitive area on her body is her brain. She needs to be emotionally aroused to fully enjoy the experience. Talk to her about what she likes, don't be afraid to try different positions, different locations and situations, use your imagination.**

Unlike us men, many women need to be stimulated in several places SIMULTANEOUSLY to reach orgasm.

When a woman gets on top, she has far greater control of the depth of penetration and rhythm, take the opportunity to arouse her emotionally with kisses, caresses of the 'girls' (her breasts), done right this will help bring her to a climax.

BUT... don't always opt for her on top position, it gets boring & tiring for her and don't forget when push comes to shove she wants you to f*ck her not the other way round.

Don't be afraid to break the silence. The sounds of pleasure that we create during love making are vibrational renditions of our emotional state. When a man and woman unite in this way the shared frequency they reach can be so intense it brings both to ecstasy.

Sex first thing in the morning is the best time for you to achieve a stronger, longer performance, you also have more energy.

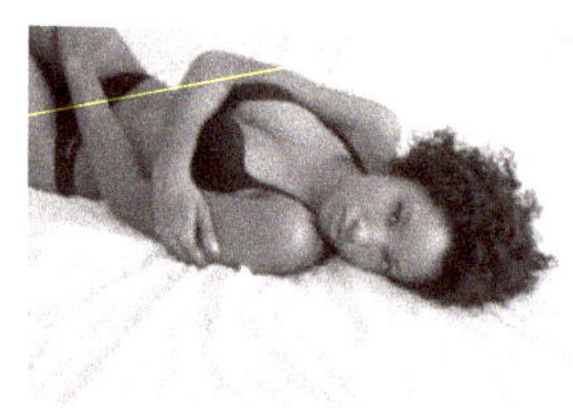

DO I HAVE TO GO DOWN (ORAL SEX)?

No. For spiritual and sometimes simply hygienic reasons many men do not want or like to engage in oral sex. Do not feel forced to reciprocate if it's not your thing.

BUT AM I A HYPOCRITE FOR WANTING HER TO GO DOWN?

No, but although spiritually they are not the same act, she may not want to for similar or even political reasons. Respect this. She may give you a good hand job instead.

ARE YOU A WANKER?

Masturbation is often treated like a joke but there are several reasons why some of us do it.

- The first, and most obvious, is sexual relief, not only for single men who want sex but are not having it, but also for those of us in stable healthy relationships. It's not often talked about but masturbation can help prevent a man with a very active sexual appetite from cheating with other women. It works by actively 'curbing' that desire until we have the discipline to do it mentally.

- It can also assist in reducing the pressure and anticipation we feel before an important meeting or occasion, in so doing, it help us maintain our cool or 'mojo'.

Don't forget, women masturbate too, some, far more often than men.

- Many experts also claim masturbation decreases the risk of prostate cancer, but some suggests that too much may increases it, especially if you're under thirty.

- Whilst ejaculating two or three times before being intimate with a woman may mean that there is less sperm being released (reducing the risk of making her pregnant) this is NOT a safe contraceptive method. The only benefit this serves is enabling you to perform for longer as you will need to work harder to achieve ejaculation again.

- Do not become a compulsive masturbator, good sex is about far more than just ejaculation. Remember the body is capable of self-regulating its sexual desires through nocturnal emission ('wet dreams').

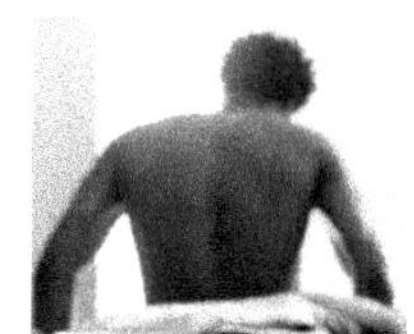

WARNING

Beware wanking addiction. Masturbation is not a substitute for sex. By its very nature masturbation often exposes us to some spiritually damaging erotic stimuli. It is important to remember that there is no legal or safe alternative that compares to the high of making love to a woman you care about. If done correctly, it's one of life's ultimate expressions of physical euphoria.

Those who enjoy a regular sex life (orgasm) are often more content with life, less stressed, more relaxed and enjoy a boost to their immunity system. Consider the fact that 390 minutes of sex can burn up to 90 calories at a time, multiply this by a few times a week and the benefits are obvious.

There are many spiritual and medical theories about what happens when a man and woman ejaculates during lovemaking. Some believe the woman releases a powerful energy which men absorb, whilst others believe the woman derives extra life and vitality by depleting the man's life force.

Practice controlling your breath as you become excited in order to redirect the energy throughout your body and not just to the love muscle. This can enable you to last hours.

Tantric sex is designed to circumvent this be learning how to achieve a whole body orgasm without ejaculating. Not only does this increase the duration of love making, but it's also believed to increase our health.

Do not feel bad if you find yourself coming too early (premature ejaculation). Some men are emotionally more sensitive than others and this can occur simply at the thought or sound (moans, motions, etc) of their partner reaching sexual climax or arousal.

This need not be embarrassing with a sensitive partner, for with will power and her support the second and third time around you should last longer and be capable of satisfying her beyond her dreams.

However what is clear is that once a man climaxes, most, upon release of that energy feel depleted and often fall asleep. Sadly, this often occurs before the woman has been satisfied. The solution therefore is to learn how to control and even halt orgasm until enough energy has been shared to satisfy both your and her needs.

If you cannot survive more than 90 seconds to ten minutes inside her vagina then practice. Masturbation is one of the best exercises you can do to learn ejaculation control, remember practice makes perfect.

If you find yourself about to climax too early, distract yourself with less exciting thoughts, try stopping and starting sexual stimulation, even withdrawing temporarily, if needed to increase the time it takes to reach climax

Try and achieve each stage in this program, not moving on to the next stage until you can complete the first consistently.

WAKACISE PROGRAM (WITH OR WITHOUT EROTIC STIMULI)

Stage 1	15 minutes without popping (Hands free)
Stage 2	15 minutes using a lubricant like baby oil or Vaseline. (Direct Contact)
Stage 3	What you waiting for? There is no stage 3, go and get her...

WHAT SIZE ARE YOU?

Average size erect is 5 - 6 inches, so if you're...

Small - it is imperative you learn extra skillz.

Medium - lucky you, just don't take her for granted.

Large - walk with confidence, but not arrogance, or she'll leave you for a medium with a smaller ego.

Extra large - this could be a problem, it is imperative you learn extra skillz, lose the arrogance or lose your friends.

CIRCUMCISION

There are many reasons to be circumcised, not only does the penis look better, but its more hygienic, provides a natural defence against HIV and is a sign of initiation (rite of passage) in many spiritual traditions. If your parents didn't circumcise you as a child you can still go through the process but it may be a little painful.

Hospitals may try and dissuade you by saying they only do it for religious reasons but don't let them scare you.

The process is likely to cost a few hundred pounds and can be carried out by an Islamic or Jewish practitioner if there is no one from your own heritage community available where you live.

WHAT SIZE IS SHE?

Never make the mistake of thinking you can tell the size of a woman's vagina by the size of her build... you can't. There are only three significant sizes/shapes and they are all relative to your size, not hers.

Tight – She may love it this way, you think you're gonna hurt her, either way she needs to recover before coming back for more, an acquired taste. Be gentle and patient, with luck you will both adapt.

Right – So smooth you're afraid to move cause you'll pop in seconds, the perfect fit.

Large – she's too big or you're too small either way no one's feeling anything (oh... and this size has nothing to do with a woman having experienced childbirth).

IMPORTANT NOTE:

It is very important to understand that she had no choice over her size and shape, just like you had no say over your length and width, or the colour of your skin. Your soul mate could just not be the 'right' fit and that is that.

It's not the end of the world, but do not compare her to an ex lover because truth be known the reason why she's an ex is probably still valid, and although sex is an important part of any relationship, as long as she makes you happy it's worth remembering that with sex it's not just what you've got, but how you and she use it that counts.

THE TROUBLE WITH CONDOMS

They stink, they're uncomfortable and they split. It's difficult to get enthusiastic about condoms, but look on the bright side. If you're about to use it, you are probably less than an hour away from some great mind blowing sex. Ask her to put it on for you by making the whole procedure a foreplay ritual. If you and she become serious, go to a clinic and get tested so that you can both go natural with confidence.

WHAT SHOULD I EXPECT FROM HER

There is this saying that what all men really want is 'a lady on the street, who is a whore in bed'. Over time the word whore has been replaced with 'freak' and the word lady with 'queen'. Freak is meant to suggest her being sexually free, queen is used to signify her being classy. Either way this still doesn't work. NEVER call your woman a whore.

A Sample of Sexual Characteristics

1 **Lazy Gal** – She looks as foine as hell, but she just lies there like she's sleeping. Puts more effort into *looking* good, than being good (you're gonna cheat on her it's inevitable).

2 **Church Gal** – Textbook love making. Not bad, but not great either, don't expect any surprises (don't give up on her, she has potential).

3 **Bad Gal** - If you're up for it, this is the one if you're only interested in is sex, she knows it all, will teach you everything you need to know and you won't be able to stop until she gets bored and dumps you. (Understanding material – let's face it you're never gonna trust her 100% with another man).

4 **Woman** - This is the woman who Fela in his song Lady refers to as being able to do 'the fire dance'. She's kind, hard working, strong and confident but when she smiles it looks as though butter wouldn't melt in her mouth. This girl is hot, she listens, learns, and even if shy, has the ability to adapt to your rhythm in order to accommodate the best for both of you. (Relationship material).

WHAT SHE'S NOT EXPECTING FROM YOU

Andrex - Soft, strong, and very very long (she crying cause you can't get it up).

Wam Bam - You spend more time looking in the mirror at yourself than her, then cum in 3 minutes flat!

Faker - You've got a fine body but a tiny penis with no skills to compensate.

Ever Ready - a man who pounds without stopping, uses the same two positions, and never checks to see if she's bored.

Relationship Tips

The good news is that you both want the same thing, loyalty, unconditional love, companionship, loyalty, a warm bed and regular sex, the problem is one of you may not realise it yet!

Knowing how to maintain a healthy relationship is just as important as knowing how to get into one.

HOW 2 KEEP HER

If she's the mushy type then on valentine's day, remember to send her a gift of flowers to her workplace followed up by dinner at a favourite restaurant or an intimate meal for two at home. If you or she are not fans of all the fuss then you may want to occasionally surprise her with a love letter in the post or a 'not because it's valentine's day' gift.

When driving or walking down the street (especially in summer), don't turn your head to look at every sexy woman you see, if you must look, then lust with your eyes only ala Terminator.

Tell her you 'adore' her until you're ready to use the love word.

Never forget her birthday or the day you met/first date/commitment. Take her out for dinner on each anniversary. Tell her it's a surprise and ask her to dress nice/sexy/casual. Make sure you are dressed well too.

Spend at least 15 minutes each day talking to her about how she's feeling. Put it in context there are 1440 minutes in a day.

Women hate when the only time you touch them is when you want sex.

When a woman talks about their feelings do not argue or get defensive with her, she may not be criticising you or trying to make a point, she's often just pondering stuff.

If you're in a bad mood tell her you want to talk about it later, don't forget or she'll think you don't want to confide in her or worse... that you're confiding in another!

Keep the romance going, send text messages or leave love notes in her pockets, shoes, etc, for no reason.

Tell her you love her at least once a month, more if she needs to hear it often to feel reassured. But ONLY say it if you MEAN it. Oh and don't say it so often it devalues the meaning, telling her 'I Love You' is your get out of jail card when the shit hits the fan, use it wisely.

Send her handwritten letters from time to time telling her how much you love her and recalling some of your favourite times together.

If you have a bad memory then make a note of her birthday, favourite colour, favourite flowers, favourite chocolates, favourite restaurant and clothes size.

Some women will hide their own needs and agree to what you want. Just because she has done this doesn't mean it's what she wants. To avoid a storm of trouble later encourage her to be honest with you.

Fantasise about her during sex, not a supermodel, film star or worse an ex girlfriend.

Buy her at least one gift every few months, they don't have to be expensive, just a sincere romantic gesture to make her feel special.

Under no circumstances put your woman on a to do list, if she finds it she will be hurt by the fact you felt the need to 'schedule' her, she doesn't like to be catalogued between pay bills and go shopping, she wants to be number one, always.

If you like computer games buy a copy of a puzzle game you can both play collaboratively, if it's competitive then let her beat you at it until she gets better.

If she's in a bad mood then the best way to get her out of it is to encourage her to talk while listening.

If you stop seeing her as sexy, then she won't feel the need to be sexy with you.

Plan a surprise romantic weekend trip away every six-twelve months (anywhere abroad or with a beach is good).

Try making her dinner or breakfast in bed every so often.

Don't lie to your woman, her natural attention to detail gives her fantastic intuition as to when you're not being truthful.

Listen and talk to your woman, if you don't someone else will.

Always respond to her texts within half an hour, it takes seconds. To not do so sends her the message that she's no longer a priority to you.

Want her to feel sexy... then ask her to go out for dinner without wearing knickers.

Try and make time to go away on a date with her ALONE, just like it was in the beginning.

A woman hates the idea of being seen as boring, if she's the only one to initiate conversations or sex then she will feel you're no longer interested in her.

Don't forget to invite her to major events with you. You may be used to being independent but she wants to know that her presence in your life is meaningful. If she's not there to get involved and share birthdays, family meals, etc, then she knows you shouldn't be there to share the same with her.

When in public, a sexy whisper in her ear ...

NEVER DO TABOOS

Never have a go at your women in front of her family or friends. The idea that you have deliberately made her feel small in front of those that know her hurts her more than you can possibly imagine.

Never stop holding her hand in public. If you only touch her in private and maintain a distance in public then this gives off the message that you're ashamed to be with her, it suggests that you're cheating and don't want to be 'caught' by someone else.

Never let money be the cause of an argument - a lack of cash often exaggerates minor issues into serious problems. The real cause of this feeling is usually a sense of insecurity. If she's overspending, then give examples through discussion of better ways to avoid waste and save cash. This is the time to pull together, share and support each other. But don't forget, even at crisis time, you both deserve some treats to make life more bearable.

Never break your intimate connection. Even during and when recovering from a disagreement it hurts. Always try and maintain eye contact and some physical contact when talking. If you can't bear to look or hold her, then why should she put up being with you.

NEVER compare her to another woman unless you're saying she is better and have a valid detailed explanation to back it up.

Tell her when she looks sexy, every clothing decision she makes from what to buy, to what to wear, how & when takes her ages, she needs to know when it works.

She loves you, you love her, you're both so content you're letting yourself slide, she gained a few pounds and so have you, only thing is that you're now starting to notice slimmer younger models and starting to question what you've got at home - Go on a diet or keep fit plan together, do joint activity sports, and increase your sex life, it's the best way to burn of excess calories together.

The biggest threat to your relationship is boredom, as a man you always feel the need for new mountains to conquer.

If she's starting to look too predictably 'wifey' then go clothes shopping with her to discover that 'new girlfriend'. Make the effort to start dating as it was at the beginning again, do role play re-enacting the moment of the first kiss.

So your children are under two and its tough sharing your best friend, you're not able to go out together or make love as frequently as usual and it's playing havoc on your nerves. Don't argue with her, work with her, she's probably feeling it too, she just handles it better.

If you have just come out of a previous relationship avoid sending any long intimate letters or emails to your ex, despite what she says, when she realises it's truly over she WILL use them against you when you reject her.

Don't ever forget how important it is that the two of you enjoy each other's company, make time to play with her and don't drop the ball.

UNDERSTANDING HER

When it comes to emotions, whilst men quantify, women typically don't, a problem is a problem there is no big or small, just all. DON'T forget this no matter what she says.

Some info is strictly on a need to know basis such as 'Which of your current friends have you slept with?' Don't answer unless she really, really needs to know.

When telling her an important story remember to give her details, the main points are NOT enough.

She likes shopping, we don't. We like lists, she doesn't. Get over it.

A little ego can make a man seem confident, a large ego can make a man seem arrogant, *no* ego can make a man seem impotent. If she has no respect for you it's over.

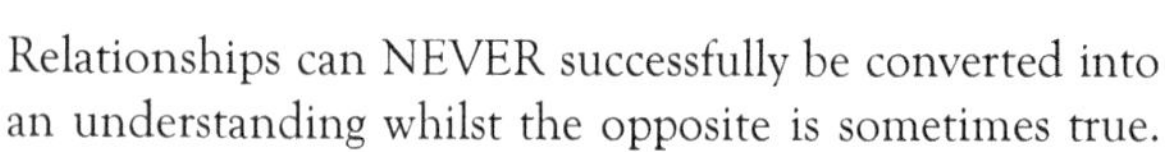

Relationships can NEVER successfully be converted into an understanding whilst the opposite is sometimes true.

If she's upset but not with you then sometimes she just needs a hug.

Six Golden Relationship Rules

1 **Love her, have fun, play together, stay together**

Remember why you're together and celebrate it. Often.

2 **Be Truthful, even if it will hurt**

Trust is the ultimate bond of any relationship. If you do not trust each other, it's all over, or soon will be.

3 **There is nothing more important than family**

Be friendly with her friends and family because they become your judge and jury when you f*ck up.

4 **Never answer a question during sex**

At the point of you coming together, you and she are one – when this happens there is no more powerful truth serum in the world.

5 **Be Sensitive**

No matter how confident she seems, never ever mention another woman's name more than twice within a 24 hour period, not even your mother, but it's ok if it's your daughter.

6 **Don't ignore her, listen**

If your girlfriend can't talk to you she WILL talk to someone else (probably about you), so be her best friend. Remember if you love her, then there are plenty of other men out there that want to do the same thing, she needs a good reason to say no.

HOW 2 LISTEN WHEN SHE'S GOING ON

Women hate to be told that they are nagging because that then by definition makes them a nag. The problem is that there are times when they do, well nag. Just like when we say the same things over and over and they just want to say 'I've got it already' but instead call us boring. Who wants to be a bore? In order to get it to stop...

Listen to her and don't interrupt while she's talking.

Let her vent, once all the anger and frustration has come out she'll start to feel better.

Be Quiet. Sometimes she just wants a fight and anything you say will lead to one.

Don't offer solutions until she asks a 'W' question (who, why, where or what) and then answer all questions in the context of "if it was me...."

Always try to take her side of an argument, remember you're her partner, so even when you don't agree with her, your job is to be honest telling her you don't agree whilst still being on her side and supporting her.

HOW 2 GET OUT OF A TOUGH ARGUMENT

- Say sorry... be sincere.
- This step is very important... STFU... just listen.

- If you raise your voice and don't listen to her, she will think you don't care about her opinion, and if you don't care about that, you can't really care about her
- Answer her questions, agree you were wrong, but DON'T ask 'w' questions or bring up the past.
- Do NOT say "I agree with you, BUT...", the 'but' part pisses her off because it negates all she has just said.
- Wait for makeup sex (do not initiate moves for at least 6 hours, it may be anytime within the next 24 hours unless you really pissed her off. Explain your view AFTER you've made her come.

IS PMS REAL?

Err... dunno, not worth the risk asking.

Healing Together

1. Both write a 'things I love about you' list

2. Both write a 'things that make me unhappy' list

3. Sit on the floor in an ash circle lit with candles, talk and listen with naked honesty (read *Spirit of Intimacy*)

PHRASES 2 BE WARY OF...

We need to talk

Answer: "OK"

(and say absolutely NOTHING else)

Answer: "That's good"

(if you're feeling devilish add 'hey.. me too')

Do you love me?

Answer: Yes.

Do you find her attractive?

Answer: She's ok, not my type though.

Hold her hand and look into her eyes.

Sorry, I really mean it

At this point it's best to just be quiet no matter what she says

~~You are right, I was~~ wrong

(but have a convincing 'why' defence ready, she aint stupid).

So how do you feel?

Do not ask this unless you have enough time to listen, nod your head when appropriate, every now and then say "I understand" and ask questions like "why do you still feel that way?" Afterwards she should be feeling better.

GIFT IDEAS

- A book on personal growth, spirituality or healing.
- A CD of her favourite music
- Flowers - ask the florist to pick a bunch with her favourite colours.
- Those cards with mushy messages or better still, buy a blank one and write your own.
- Never underestimate the power of chocolate (cakes, sweets, hearts, body paint, etc).
- Mail her some tickets to an event (favourite singer, new play, eg).
- Always wrap her presents up, it adds to the mystery.
- A gift voucher for one 'all expenses paid' day at her favourite hairdresser, health or beauty spa.
- Poetry (especially if you've written it yourself).

How 2 Answer...

Words are powerful, as a man it is imperative to understand that silence is often the best weapon, but for in those instances where you must speak, then always try to be honest but exercise caution.

THE 'HOW DO I LOOK?' QUESTION

The best answer is the simple "You look beautiful"

NICE (also sweet) is for when you neither like it nor dislike it.

SEXY (also hot) is for when you want to undress and take her right now.

OK (also good) is for when she could visit your parents AND go to work in it.

PRETTY is for when she loves it, but you think it's boring.

SOPHISTICATED & CLASSY is for when you love it but she thinks it's boring.

GOOD (also cute) is a polite way of saying she looks hot without being overly sexy

GREAT (also cool) is for when you love it and she looks happy in it.

THE 'DO I LOOK FAT IN THIS?' QUESTION

Sigh... the big butt, large thighs and the quest for the perfect body dilemma...

Firstly remember, no matter what you tell her she'll still think she needs to lose weight. DO NOT mention the word 'fat' EVER. The correct answer is always;

> "Of course not".

However, If she does make her look fat then answer;

> "No, but it looks a bit cheap"

Or

> "No, but it doesn't do you justice".
>
> (IMPORTANT: Avoid answering why?)

Or

If you really hate it then answer;

> "No, but it looks like something my ex would wear".

THE 'ARE MY BREASTS TOO SMALL?' QUESTION

You answer this one VERY carefully. Some women can obsess over their breast size, especially if they know that you are physically attracted to women whose form is suitably curvaceous.

The safest answer is one of the classics:

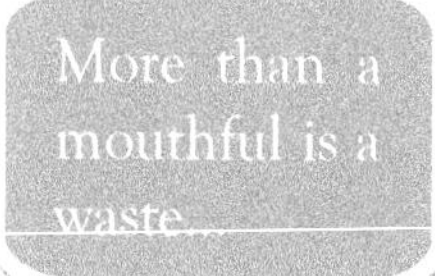

I love you just the way you are...

Truth of the matter is if it really bothered you she wouldn't be with you, but it's unlikely you'll be able to convince her 100%.

Remember socially, a woman's breast is just like a mans' penis, size matters but in the case of a woman hers is permanently on display, so it's easier for her to feel inadequate when surrounded by other women who are more naturally endowed.

Imagine if everybody could see the size of our equipment while clothed... the world would probably be a very different place.

THE "DOES MY BUM LOOK BIG?" QUESTION

Your job as a man is to encourage her to love herself. When she puts herself down she's implying you've got bad taste!

Answer: Yes! It's supposed to, then find and tell her to read the "behind every great woman" article in the June 2002 issue of the Oprah magazine, and then play her the video of 'baby got back' by Sir Mix-a-lot!

Ask her to do that hypnotic dance where you are mesmerised by her ass.

If she feels her portions are too modest, the next time you are being intimate hold her from behind and remind her that you love all her curves, even the ones she can't see.

Attitude

The current myth perpetuated by idiots is that sistas are feisty, cheeky, loud mouthed materialistic, only good for sex, baby making, female dogs.

The simple truth is that this is a lie.

They are simply women who because society often places them on the bottom rung of the social scale, many have had to learn to be assertive to get the message across that they will no longer be abused.

Weaves

The current myth is that sistas who wear a weave (not braids) have either lost their cultural identity or are not Africentric.

The Truth is that the majority of them do it to feel attractive, not only for themselves, but also for us men. Not just because it's easier to maintain as they claim, but in response to the constant media images attacking and portraying their natural selves as ugly, whilst praising their 'relaxed', fake long flowing shoulder length hair selves as beautiful.

From plastic dolls to video vixens in music videos, this message demanding women conform to the straightening of their hair is everywhere. Sadly many choose to give up on their natural beauty and wear the dead hair of other people as a response to us men who have fallen for this fake illusion of 'universal' beauty.

Even language perpetuates the beauty myth, gorgeous African locs (twists) become 'dread' locks whilst a blond 'bombshell' is known as 'Goldilocks'

In short, too many of our sistas have sadly rejected a crucial part of their own heritage by adapting their looks in order to blend into society and keep us interested.

There is nothing wrong in women wearing weaves as a fashion statement, but when it is a deliberate denial of self it is ultimately soul destroying and destructive to the self esteem of younger women.

Therefore, our job as men is to encourage and awaken their inner confidence by letting them know that it is their natural self we find beautiful, not the fake cosmetics.

Weaves, yes they're hideous and can make her head look big from the back but as long as the female toupee is in fashion, you're fighting against the case of the emperor's new clothes (it used to be wigs!)

Skin Colour

Western society encourages us to believe that the lighter the colour of our skin, the more attractive we are. So called 'super' models and pop entertainers are encouraged to wear blond weaves and those of us with light brown skin are disproportionately presented as the only acceptable alternative to the beauty ideal.

Women never forget what we say about the looks of other women. It could be an actress, a neighbour, someone at work or a sista on road. From the moment we mention "women we find attractive" her name and/or body type is permanently added to a list of potential threats.

This has a detrimental effect on those of us with beautiful rich complexions whilst the damage done to the self esteem and confidence of young children is immeasurable.

Some use toxic skin whitening products to 'bleach' their skin, others put on too much makeup to mask psychological damage that has led them to believe everything whiter is 'fairer' and anything with African features (including self) is ugly.

Nonetheless, it is important not to give negative focus to those who are naturally lighter skinned, including those of us that are born with dual heritage. Instead we must still recognise the beauty in our diversity and challenge those that abuse this 'fair skin beauty' bias as well as the system that maintains it.

This 'ugly' dark skin mantra is obviously nonsense but the stereotype is so pervasive it affects hundreds of millions each year who due to cultural disinheritance risk their health to match this ideal or consistently chose partners based not on looks or personality but often on a subconscious ideology promoting of 'white is right'.

Whilst we all have our preferences, don't get mixed up in supporting the school of thought that says all of a woman's beauty is in her hair, or her breasts. Women have enough challenges without us adding this into the mix.

HOW DO I KNOW SHE'S THE ONE

You may not fancy your "perfect" mate at first, but you'll be attracted to her. Give it time and you'll be confused as to how you missed her little perfect imperfections the first time round.

- She'll know the intimate, emotionally naked you and still be your best friend. You'll value her opinion of you above anyone else, and to see HER hurt causes YOU pain.

- Honesty is the best policy, if you instinctively don't trust her then she's not the one. Period.

- She always knows what to say and do to make you feel better when the world feels like its closing in.

- You miss her five minutes after she leaves or finishes talking to you.

- When you don't feel that you've compromised yourself by being in a relationship with her.

- If a year after you first met her your heart still beats fast or you get excited whenever she rings or sends you a message.

- She defends you in public even when she knows you're wrong AND corrects you in private.

- She won't let you leave the house looking a state without mentioning or doing something about it.

- She doesn't go mad when she OCCASIONALY catches you looking at other women (she aint happy about it though).

She gets uncomfortable with the idea of you going out with an Ex, but trusts you enough not to make a big deal about it.

(Don't do it often, no more than once a year)

- If you still love being around her when sex is not possible (life's a b*tch sometimes).

- She's cool with you having female friends, as long as you're cool with her having male ones (don't betray that trust).

You know she's the one when despite all your little faults, she still feels you're perfect for her and you know she is perfect for you.

- When you finally realise that you there will always be better *looking* alternatives around, but none that will make you feel as beautiful inside as she does.

- You love her, she loves you. Unconditionally.

THE LIST (Stuff You Need To Know About Her)

Sometimes it's useful to approach the decision to start a long term relationship like an employer with a job application form.

- What are her spiritual views?
- When she smiles does it make you want to smile?
- Does she listen?
- Is she a loyal person, why did she split from ex?
- What about honesty and ethics? Would she have an affair if the man she loved became disabled?
- Is she sensitive and supportive? What's her attitude towards men who are broke whilst out looking for work?
- Is she considerate? Punctual? Reliable?
- Is she sensible for times when there's no cash?
- Is she family orientated? Does she like children?
- Does she cook? What are her views on motherhood and traditional roles?
- Does she have initiative? If there is a problem does she help try to solve it or always wait for you?

HOW DO I KNOW SHE'S NOT THE ONE

Sex is great, you like her, but you've got that feeling in your gut that you don't really want to introduce her to your friends or family.

Snooper – She looks through your stuff at every given opportunity without asking. Instant dismissal.

Digger - Money is often a serious issue between you.

Moaner - The moment she leaves you alone, you call up a friend to cheer you up.

Fatal – She wants to know all your friends, your every movement and calls if you're five minutes late.

Playarette – She only visits or wants you to call at certain times.

Miss Thang - When you're with her all you want to do is have sex, but when she talks you realise you don't actually like her. Sorry, but you're not in love, you're in lust with her.

HELP... SHE WANTS ME TO WAIT FOR SEX

- If you know she's not the one then set yourself a time limit and move on if it expires. If however you think she COULD be the one, then wait. DO NOT sleep (or tell her you slept) with someone else while waiting. Avoid temptation from other female friends who are interested.

HELP... SHE WANTS TO MOVE IN

- Does she respect your privacy? Have the two of you been physically intimate? Have you had that first big argument? If so, how did you resolve it? Does she keep bringing up past issues and could you live with that behaviour first thing in the morning?

- Living together is as personal as it gets. Yes, it gives you permanent access to the one you love, but it also exposes both of your flaws. If you're not ready for this step then first try letting her sleep over a few days in the week and see how it feels. Ask her to bring some stuff over so that she can change for work or whatever from yours without having to go back to hers. Go food shopping together and see what the process is like.

- If after six – nine months things are still cool (in fact they should be better than cool) then discuss the idea of moving in *together.* Try going on holiday together. You may have found the woman you should marry.

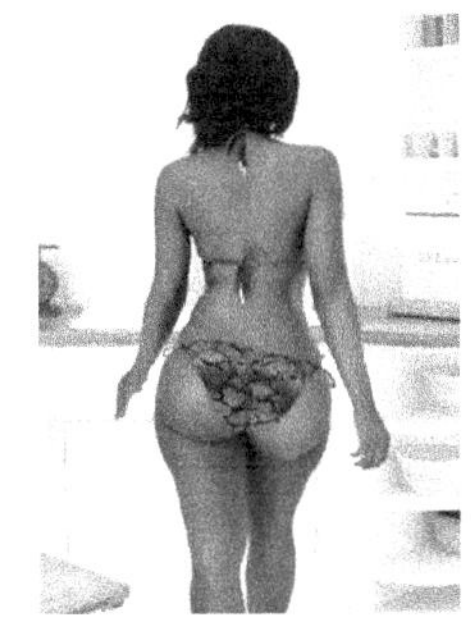

It's impossible to be a good father without love, discipline and a working relationship with the child's mother. Therefore the best scenario is to be married or in a stable long term relationship where the children feel the love of both parents on a daily basis. If as parents you fall out, the children must NEVER be used as a weapon to get back at the other party. Their happiness and emotional wellbeing must be placed before yours, especially whilst they are still young.

Infants

- Alternate late night feeds with your partner.
- If your child is a baby then make sure that, at the very least that you know how to change their nappies, prepare their milk/feed and wash/bathe them.
- Always read your children a story at bedtime to help them off to sleep.

Education

- Always attend parents' evenings at school.
- Try to attend all school play and trips your child may be involved with.
- LISTEN to your children, ask about their day at school and listen carefully to what they have to say.

- Check their homework and take them to the library every week.

Development

- Many children wet their beds, don't punish them for it. Just encourage them to always tell you so the sheets can be changed and their skin washed.
- Teach them about their history and culture, normalise the lessons.

Children must contribute to doing household chores. Cleaning, washing up, and making their own beds, washing clothes. Do NOT pay them for this work.

- Ask your children to read a book to you every week.
- Encourage them to write poems and draw pictures as a way to express themselves.
- Take your child to a martial arts class (eg. Mashufaa, Qigong, Capoiera, etc)
- Discuss the Ancestors and spirituality every week.
- Teach them to ride a bike
- Teach them to swim
- Teach them to play Chess and Oware

- Encourage their creativity through art. Have fun.
- Be strict but fair AND flexible.

Wellbeing and emotional security

- Tell them you love them every day, kiss and hug them without giving any particular reason.
- As well as being their parent, you are your children's best friend, their major backup in any argument, remember this and back them up, don't ever let them feel alone.
- Listen to them. Some of their concerns may seem trivial but they are huge to them.
- Always remain united as parents when it comes to your children's emotional wellbeing, do not argue or disrespect each other in front of them.

Social

- Do NOT buy your children expensive designer clothes unless for a very special treat or birthday present after a year of hard work.
- Learn the names of all your child's friends and enemies that may bully them.

Hint: Try and remember your children's birth weight, and how long labour was... women love to hear that kind of stuff.

Commitment

- If you don't live with your children then call at LEAST once a week and visit them at LEAST every fortnight.
- Don't be late without calling.
- If you're not married to your child's mother, then make sure you both sign a parental responsibility agreement.

GETTING MARRIED

Marriage for many of us men is a scary institution. Some of us fear making the wrong decision and being committed to a single person for the rest of our lives.

- Do not confuse the nightmare of planning a wedding with the reality of being married. Whilst the events leading up to the ceremony can be very stressful, the end result of being a husband and having a wife is priceless.

Marriage is the traditional way that young people express to the world they are grownups ready to take the next step into adulthood.

- Marriage is the ultimate romantic and practical means to provide security and stability for you and your family unit.

- If you are living contently with a woman after three years despite the ups and downs, if you still love her and can see yourself being together for many more years then get married. This is especially so if you have children or plan to have children together.

"No matter how much I love her, I'm just not sure I can be faithful to one woman for the rest of my life."

Excellent, deep down she feels the same but is smart enough to keep it to herself. Being honest with yourself in this way is a clear sign of emotional maturity. It means you are ready to face the realities of life. Remember, there's no rule saying you can't have female friends, just that your wife is number one.

"Why risk breaking our relationship it, if it's already working as it is"

To keep it working. Love alone is not enough. Marriage provides security and protection from outside threats and pressures. Having someone to share life's many gifts and burdens also gives you a confidence like no other. There are few words to explain the feeling that comes from knowing you have someone in your corner who is not a blood relative, but still loves and stands by you no matter how bad things get.

"Why bother, we've been together for a few years and already have a child"

Marriage is still the best cultural (and legal) institution we have for providing a stable loving home for our children to grow up with the benefits of two parents.

ONE WOMAN FOR LIFE? (THE TEMPTATION OF NEWNESS)

The question that worries you is can you be faithful to one woman for the rest of your life? Have you made the right decision?

The first thing to learn is that you will always be attracted to beautiful women, just as she will feel the same about other men. The 'newness' that comes with learning about someone we find attractive is addictive. The trick is to value your relationship so much that you develop the discipline not to act on opportunities that can risk breaking it.

Other women will be attracted to you the moment you are in a stable relationship, some will even actively pursue you. They can often sense your contentment, and your lack of sexual hunger - it makes you stand out above all the single guys out there. Yet whilst it can be intoxicating and very faltering to the ego, if you do not have a strong enough will to say no, it can cost you both your true love and the new woman.

Ultimately, if you're not sure about getting married, or feel pressured to do so then don't do it. Wait until you're both ready. Just be careful not to leave it so long (over seven years) or you may find out that she decides you're not serious and leaves you.

Men often fall in lust faster than women fall in love, this sometimes means unless we are attracted to her character we lose interest quick once the thrill of the chase has worn off. If you've dated her for a while but now you want out then...

THE TOP FIVE REASONS/EXCUSES

1. "it's me, not you"
2. "fear of commitment"
3. "I'm not ready for a relationship"
4. "I fell in lust, not in love"
5. "I still haven't got over my ex"

Do not send her a text message ending it. If you've not yet been intimate and she's not getting subtle hints in your conversation then slowly avoid her calls.

If you've already been intimate with her then it's important to be man enough to be honest, talk to her face to face and be kind. She will want to know why, have an answer. None of them will be good enough but it helps give her closure.

DEALING WITH THE PAIN OF SPLITTING UP

The pain of splitting up with someone you love is virtually identical to that of bereavement and unlike any other you will ever experience. It will make you extremely unstable, emotionally vulnerable, spiritually violated and unable to function without risk of physical and mental breakdown at anytime, anywhere.

THE SEVEN STAGES

1. DENIAL - "this can't be happening to me"
2. FEAR (cause of denial) - "how will I survive"
3. ANGER - "why me, what have I done to deserve this"
4. BARGAINING (due to guilt) - "I should have done this or said that"
5. GREIVING (leads to depression) - "I give up – I can't go on anymore, what's the point"
6. ACCEPTANCE - "I deserve happiness, I need to get to know myself again"
7. REBIRTH/RECOVERY – "I am changing my attitude and moving on with my life"

The symptoms of bereavement are: stress, lack of sleep, restlessness, tearfulness, lack of purpose, insecurity, inability to cope, Panic attacks anxiety, exhaustion.

If you recognise any of these in you, please seek help. The only healer for this pain is time. It is important you talk to a trusted family member or friend until you release all the angst. You will need to consciously sever all contact with the ex until you are able to cope with seeing or hearing from them again. It can take years but you will learn how to forgive but never forget.

> **"Love that we cannot have is the one that lasts the longest, hurts the deepest and feels the strongest..."**
>
> **An African Proverb**

Engage yourself in positive activities. If you are a creative person write, draw, sing, and dance. You can also join social groups that work in an area you have interest. Take up a physical activity, martial art or sport. You may never forget the pain of the loss, but you will learn to live with it... in time.

Health, Style and General Tips

A good woman will not let you go outside looking a mess. Be thankful, she's not nagging, she just cares about your health as well as how others see you. A good woman is confident that even when you look fine and other women hit on you, you will always come back to her. As we get older we become more content and happy with our partner, especially if married. Yet, instead of maintaining pride in our fitness and appearance, many of us get too comfortable and stop looking after how we look. This is not recommended, not just because there are always other men out there looking to have what we have (i.e. her) but also because it leads to poor health and low self-esteem.

I'M FINISHED WITH JUNK, NOW WHAT SHOULD I MUNCH

This is a list of foods that collectively help reduce blood pressure, lower cholesterol, assist the body defend against prostate cancer, fight heart diseases and increase insulin efficiency.

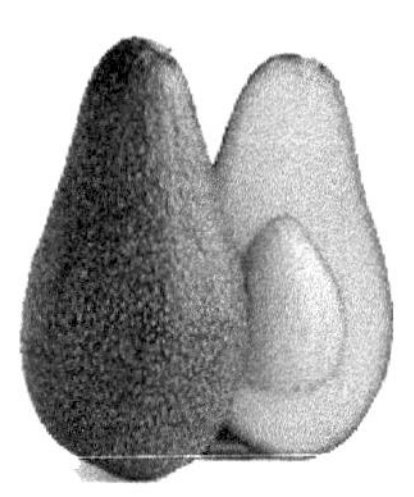

- Apples, Banana, Avocado, Water Melon, Grapes.
- Spinach, Celery, Lentils, Onions, Carrots, Red Pepper.
- Wholemeal Pasta & Rice
- Tomatoes
- Potatoes
- Garlic, Ground cinnamon
- Chick Peas, various Beans, Mushrooms.
- Wholegrain Bread, Mixed nuts, various Fruit Juices, Fruit & Fibre based cereals
- Fish (including tuna, sardines, mackerel, herring)
- Olive Oil

HOW 2 BE FIT (AKA HEALTH TIPS)

- Drink water... lots of it.
- Avoid all types of smoking (passive included).

- Never get drunk.
- No red meat.
- If you must consume dairy products then change to low fat skimmed milk.
- No chocolate, fizzy drinks or fried foods, except as an occasional treat
- If you're looking to lose weight then try drinking two glasses of water BEFORE each meal.
- Always try to pick low fat products.
- Cut down on fruit juices, too much sugar is bad for your teeth.
- Go swimming at least twice a month.
- Avoid lifts, use the stairs instead.
- Try exercising in fresh air spaces and engaging in contact sports like ball games or martial arts.

- Brush your teeth at least twice a day. Try flossing at least twice a week (it's not for everyone).

Remember whilst a gym may give you a fit looking body, there's nothing worse than being a wimp that can't run to catch a bus.

- Wash your equipment every day, check your balls for lumps, remember, you're not wanking you're looking for signs of prostate cancer!

  NOTE: a better way is to get your girlfriend to check for you.

- Be active, if you don't walk a lot then try to do some morning press ups each day. Start at 25 aim for 50 plus, then do 2 minutes worth of crunches, followed by 2 minutes worth of squats.

HOW 2 BE CLEAN

Every man must adhere to basic levels of hygiene. No woman, no matter how much she likes or even loves you will forever remain loyal and committed if you cannot get this right.

- Cut your fingernails, keep them clean.
- Please WASH your duvet cover and sheets. NOW.
- If you're drawing her bath, make sure it's clean first.

NOTE: If she seems to be spending some time in your bathroom it could be because she must change her undies everyday, if she's staying over at your place then she must wash them overnight so they're dry next morning.

SWEAT AND BODY ODOUR

If like lots of men you suffer from excess body sweat then you need to work to manage the odour.

- Body odour (B.O) is caused by the bacteria created when our perspiration mixes with the sweat glands on our bodies in particular our armpits, groin and feet.

- Sweat in itself doesn't smell, in fact our body perspires to cool itself down and get rid of toxins. But when it interacts with the oils and chemicals on our skin it can create the characteristic smell known as B.O. Therefore even our diet can affect the condition as our skin excretes chemicals of foods with strong spices.

- No matter how clean we are, the clothes we wear also retains the smell from the sweat we produced the day before. For this reason it is important to change what we wear every day and wash our clothes in a high temperature. Bacteria can survive in damp clothing so it is important to dry clothes straight way.

If you sweat a lot then you may need to shower two to three times a day. Remember you may have become accustomed to your own smell and no longer notice it but others are not.

- Some men successfully use antiperspirants such as roll-ons and sprays that block the body's ability to sweat, but for others whose skin is more sensitive this can make the problem worse and irritate the skin.

- Carry a handkerchief, flannel or small towel

- Deodorants attempt to mask the smell with a fragrance, but in Truth this is only of use after you have thoroughly washed the body's sweat glands with soap.

- Shaving your armpits is one way to reduce the space bacteria can produce odour.

TOILET HYGIENE

- If you're a skid marks in the toilet kinda brotha, then clean up before you exit.
- She always wants the seat down, so after you pee don't leave the toilet seat wet if you don't lift it up. Wipe your things and clean the seat or she'll think you're weird not being able to aim straight (don't even try to explain, she won't understand cause she's not a man).
- Never leave monsters in the toilet, get the brush and evict them. ALWAYS check after flushing the loo.
- NEVER pee in the shower, you're a man not a boy who can't hold it.
- Use the cubicles in public toilets and always wash your hands.

GETTING THINGS DONE (ACHIEVING SUCCESS)

- Be organised, make lists if necessary
- Don't procrastinate, do it now.
- Have courage and initiative, fear is your enemy.
- Keep a paper diary or filofax so you don't forget important events, people and appointments.
- Know your limits, be confident, but don't promise more than you can deliver
- Don't be ignorant, if you don't know, ask.
- Be disciplined, work hard, don't cheat
- Be true, be guided by spirit in everything you do
- Educate yourself, go to university or work under a knowledgeable mentor/role model as a volunteer.
- Learn to socialise, networking helps us find likeminded people to help us achieve our purpose.
- Find a competent partner (business or otherwise) and become best friends. Everything is easier to achieve with a little help.
- Be imaginative, creative and intelligent.
- Love self, but challenge ego.
- Be loyal, sharing and trustworthy
- Find a good woman, settle down and make a home with her.

HOW 2 LOOK STYLISH (WITHOUT GOING BROKE)

Do's

First remember you get what you pay for so don't be too cheap, nothing on this list (except possibly the coats & jackets) should cost more than £100, in fact most should be sub £50.

- Jeans or Cargo type work trousers
- A pair of plain black trainers (any more must have a specific purpose)
- Some canvas shoes and sandals
- A white shirt
- Single breasted coat
- Single breasted black Jacket
- A few casual t-shirts (without tacky images or slogans)
- Some sleeveless t-shirts for working out or hot days
- Linen Jacket
- Contrary to popular belief men don't have to wear blue, but should never wear pink. Ever.
- Going bald? Be a man and shave it all off, only the desperate cling to the final evidence of their youth.

- No Toupees (unless you still disagree with not wearing pink), if you must, wear a hat.
- A three blade razor
- Minimal jewellery (preferable handmade)
- No earrings or studs. You're a man not a girl.
- At least three sets of traditional / cultural attire.
- Wear a belt, baggy trousers that rest on your hips make you look stupid, not cool.

If your hair line is residing you have one of three choices. Accept it with confidence, restyle it in a manner that masks the issue (not recommended) or shave it all off. Hats, toupees and transplants are not options.

- Shades, but not so dark that no-one can see your eyes through them.
- A plain tie.
- Unless you are a spiritual Rasta or over two years old and under twenty eight - don't braid your hair.
- Scruffy can be cool, natural or sporty if it's clean. Dirty is just dirty, no exception.

Don'ts

Clothes manufacturers pay celebrities millions to wear clothes with their name & logo splashed all over them, unless you've got a major sponsorship deal don't be a fool and advertise for free. Buy clothes from chains with a style you like who can use their bulk purchasing power to get a good deal, NO tacky on body labelled designer clothes.

- No y-fronts or briefs – boxers, slips or tangas only.
- No thermal vests or undies
- No Pyjamas (in summer)
- No duffle coats (unless you disagree with not wearing pink).
- Skull caps and bandanas look cheap.
- Only wear hats (but not a hood) in cold weather.
- If possible DON'T walk with a bag unless it is carrying something important or something that won't fit in your pockets, women 'wear' bags, men carry them.
- If you must wear a watch then remember its number one function is to tell the time and MAYBE give you the date.
- No bow ties.
- Most permanent tattoos are now seen as 'tramp stamps' or signs of weak minded westerners adorned with cattle branding stating they are the property of

China. In very rare cases some stamps can 'look' cool, but not if it's the name of an ex or profanity. If you really feel you must get a tattoo then instead of branding yourself as a porn star or criminal, make it African, like a meaningful Adinkra symbol.

- Minimal jewellery, no earrings, medallions or sovereign rings. Avoid the pimp rapper/Mr T look like the plague... she will.

STUFF U SHOULD KNOW

- Read, write and do basic maths (including timetables 1-12)
- At least the basics of two card games (e.g. blackjack, poker)
- The history of your Ancestors
- How to drive even if you DONT have a car
- Ride a bike
- Change a plug
- Basic car maintenance (oil, water, check and change a tyre, fuses)
- Have a working knowledge of Oware and Chess (i.e. know the names and moves of all the pieces).
- Play a musical instrument
- How to cook (rice, pasta, potatoes, plantain, fish, pepper stew, soup and a tomato based sauce).
- If you're crap at flirting then practice online (Facebook, chat room, etc). Learn how to be subtle but confident, understated but with a presence.
- Location of one intimate local African/Caribbean restaurant with good quality reasonably priced food
- The location of one restaurant in a reasonably high profile area (you're really there to allow her to show off for the night and not for the tiny food portions).

- Learn what star sign you are even if you believe it's all rubbish
- Be computer literate (email, office suite of programs)
- The basic language and cultural practices of your parents
- Become an average pool player
- Avoid daytime TV. Period.
- How to wash clothes by hand
- Fan or fanatic? Keep sports in perspective
- How to do a tie
- How to research, debate using critical thought and present a strong argument competently

HOW TO SHAVE

- Electric razors are for wimps and can even *cause* bumps when used on curly hair. Use a blade. You can save yourself the cost and mess of shaving gel if you want and use plain soap mixed into a lather, but if you get bumps use a gel and aftershave.
- Beards and moustaches can unnecessarily age you. This is cool if you keep them trimmed but if you choose to let them grow uncontrollably the give you an appearance of uncouthness.

STUFF U SHOULD OWN

- Toolbox: A workbench, carpenters pencil, masking and duct tape, spirit level, clamp, 5m tape measure, hacksaw, wood saw, set of screwdrivers, Stanley knife
- Torch (Maglight)
- A camera that can record quality video images
- An up to date Passport.
- WD 40
- Cordless Drill
- Claw Hammer
- Road atlas, A to Z (Streetfinder)
- A dictionary
- Jumper cables and battery charger (if you have a car)
- Pre Pay Credit Card (with at least £100 emergency cash on it)
- A vision and integrity
- A computer (a desktop or portable PC for work and a games console for entertainment)
- A library card
- A mobile phone (with camera, internet and radio)
- Books on law, health, history and culture

STOP AND SEARCH - KNOW YOUR RIGHTS

'Stop and Search' formerly known as 'the sus laws' is an oppressive tool used by British Police forces. It allows racist officers to harass and humiliate innocent people in public and secure their DNA samples for the government's criminal database.

1. The Stop

Why am I being Stopped?

Stop and Search powers are only legal when there are used with reasonable grounds*. If you are stopped on the street by any police officer ask why? If they claim you fit the description of someone who has committed an offence then ask for reasons why they are stopping you.

2. The Grounds

What are your grounds for suspecting me? What is the description?

An officer must have objective and reasonable grounds* (unless under Sec 44, 60) to stop and detain you. This means they must believe an offense has been committed and have a good reason why they suspect you of being responsible. Before doing a search they can question you to investigate that suspicion. Every officer has discretion as to whether they exercise the power of arrest. If you refuse to answer their questions you could be detained.

3. The Questions

As I understand it, if I am not a suspect, I don't need to tell you my name

Remember, less is more. Your name is not needed if they do not suspect you of an offence. If their suspicion is eliminated through questioning you or other circumstances, they must let you know you are free to leave. Police officers are not allowed to stop you in order to find grounds to justify a search.

I don't wish to consent to the search, which power are you using,
is it PACE 1984?

4. The Search

If the officer is intent on searching you without just cause then let them know you do not consent before they proceed.

The law on Stop and Search (Police And Criminal Evidence Act 1984) states the police can only search you for;

- A prohibited article (offensive weapon, 'controlled' drugs, etc)
- Items likely to be used to commit an offence (burglary, theft, etc)
- A stolen item

5. The Record

I would like a record of this search, your name, badge number and the name of your police station

Remember, the officer has a duty to make a record of the search. You are entitled to a copy of that record from the officer on the spot (unless impractical) and up to 12 months of the incident.

IMPORTANT:
Take note of the officers name, number & the station they are attached to, also the date, time and location of the incident. Look for witnesses and ask for their contact details. Write down a full account of what happened as soon as you get a chance.

6. Helping Others

I am observing, not obstructing

If the police are acting unlawfully by abusing someone else then you are entitled to observe what is happening. It is not illegal to take a photograph with a camera or camera phone. This could later become crucial evidence. If an officer tries to stop you from watching try not to get so close that they can claim you are obstructing them from carrying out their duty. If they ask your name and details then if you want to report any abuse consider giving it to them, and state you want to be noted as a witness. That way they have to write it down. Ask for their details and make an official complaint.

- The search is unlawful if the officer is using racist bias to target you. All police officers should be willing to answer your questions.

- There are two separate powers that the police often use to mask illegal racist behaviour, Section 60 and Section 44 of the Terrorism Act. In both instances police officers are enabled by law to stop and search innocent people without reasonable grounds of suspicion.

- These specific laws enable officers to demand the removal of 'articles' of terrorism such as headgear, footwear, outer clothing or gloves. It also allows for officers to feel around and inside collars, socks and shoes and search hair.

- Failure to submit to the search amounts to an offence punishable by imprisonment or a fine or both. Intimate searches should not be done on streets. Unless using anti-terrorism powers (Sec. 44), officers are not authorised to remove your outer coat, jacket or gloves.

STUFF U SHOULD HAVE AT HOME

- A packet of condoms
- Shower mixer tap or electric shower
- Duvet & clean sheets
- Non electronic games such as Oware, Chess, Scrabble and Four in a row
- Dimmer switches
- A radio and widescreen TV
- A computer with internet access
- CD or mp3 player
- A book collection including core texts on African history and culture.

HOW 2 BE COOL

Okay truth is I can't really help you here, all I can do is give you some hint and tips that may help. Cool comes in many different forms and is not the same thing as being funny or popular.

DEFINITIONS OF COOL

Original Cool

The word cool is believed to have come from the name of a Nigerian ruler named 'Ewure' in the early 15th century. At the time his name literally translated into 'it is cool'. Not sure how true all this is but it is cool.

Classic Cool

A man who listens well, is a man everyone wants to talk to. Simply learn to shut up and listen without being judgemental

Modern Cool

Are you funny? Can you make people laugh without making someone else cry? It's a skill which makes people popular.

Pseudo Cool

Are you hip? Do you only wear designer labels and drive a 'flash wheels'. Do you find saying 'wassup' funny? Sorry but you're simply a legend in your own mind.

Rules of Cool

- 'Hip' is not cool
- Most people perceive those who are chilled as cool, hot is popular, hot is not cool
- You can buy 'hip' (think trendy) but not cool
- You can look cool but be a fool
- You can look a fool but be cool

Rules of Uncool

- Wearing shades inside or in any dark place (eg. the tube or a club).
- Poor attempts at using 'hip' cultural slang rendering them into naff phrases like 'bling', 'yo', 'wassup', 'booty', etc or adding the word 'man', 'cool', 'you know what I'm saying' after every sentence.
- Mobile phones with novelty rings.
- Showing off keys with an expensive 'sports car' key fob
- Name dropping 'famous' people you've met or know.

- There is nothing more important than family, protect them at all costs.
- Make a choice and stick to it.
- When there's no space for compromise remember it's all or nothing.
- NEVER EVER hit a woman or child (unless to stop someone from injury or in an extreme case of self defence).

Accept responsibility for ALL your actions – the good, bad and ugly.

- Accept responsibility for ALL your actions.
- Don't cheat on your woman.
- Be assertive, it's not the same as being aggressive.
- Be imaginative, in life there is no spoon,,,
- Walk with your head up, don't avoid eye contact with anyone.
- Don't be a bully, never pick a fight with someone weaker than you.
- Avoid all physical confrontation, (practice by not killing flies). However feel free to DEFEND yourself with force if it comes down to them or you.

HOW 2 BE A MATE

This section only refers to 'man to man relationships'. Please watch the film 'When Harry met Sally' PRIOR to attempting male/female 'mates'. It is possible, but often difficult. As with all friendships, honesty is the key.

General

- NEVER ever let money come between you.
- Always avoid his weak spots.
- Don't let him be the only one who calls.

- Your fights are your fights, so don't involve him.
- Return what you borrow, replace what you break.
- Don't sulk, its ugly.

Women

- Never attempt to steal his potential date.
- When he's talking to the pretty one, you talk to her ugly friend.
- Never screw a friend to screw a girl.
- Never 'share' a girlfriend

Relationships

- Never interfere in an argument between him and his woman.
- Don't take the piss out of his partner even when he does.

Ex's

- Try not to go out with his ex.
- Try not to slag her off, cause he may go back to her...

Support

- When he's opening up and going all mushy, shut up, listen and never tease him about crying.
- Cover for him unconditionally, but always tell him if he's wrong.
- Call him when he's hurting, visit him if he's not answering.
- Don't take advantage when he's down.

Her Rules*

Some women have rules in their head telling her how to act when dealing with men. This practise that has been going on for years is transmitted between grandmothers, aunties, mothers, daughter and sisters even till this day. Many of these include ideas that in the passing down across the generations have not been updated or modified to deal with the reality of today. As such some of the make sense whilst others do not.

To find and have a decent chance of having any kind of relationship with that perfect woman you need to understand them. Here are some of the rules many women use to trap us;

"Don't talk to a man first (and don't ask him to dance)"

Whilst there are women that will break this rule, in most instances it remains your place to man up and approach her first. Remember, every woman likes it when a man attempts to flirt with them, even if she appears a bit frosty at first.

"Be a creature unlike any other"

It doesn't matter what your friends think, it is YOU that must find her special. Because of the mass availability and cheapness of body technology such as hair extensions (weaves), most women can recreate a reasonable copy of the plastic 'look' seen in music videos and TV adverts. Be careful, we are often taken in by the attractiveness on the outside when what really matters is that she is beautiful on the inside.

"Don't stare at men"

She wants you to notice her. But hold on – NO - that doesn't mean you are free to give her the psycho stare, instead catch her eye and if she doesn't turn away then give her a gentle smile. Note however, if you and her are starting to flirt with the eyes then under no circumstances repeat the same action with another woman in the same space.

"Don't meet him halfway or go dutch on a date"

Even if it will make you broke, pay the whole bill on the first few dates. This rule remains true irrespective of whether she's earning more money than you. Don't make a big deal of it but understand that this gesture helps her know you value her. Some women may insist on paying their own way because they don't like the idea of being 'bought'. In these cases it's ok to make a fuss but if she's still insistent let her contributes but remember... no matter what she says, most women desire and appreciate a man who can take care of them – physically, emotionally and financially. She's not planning going straight back to work the week following delivery of your babies!

"Don't call him and rarely return his calls"

This is a tired play on the old "treat them mean to keep them keen" mantra. If she carries on with this then drop her. While it's true that women should be able to play a little hard to get, it is important to know that she's not playing games. Refusing to call or return your calls just to make you anxious is simply rude.

"Always end phone calls first"

The old maxim 'less is more' tends to work for everything. If you're having a great discussion on the phone, imagine what it would be like in person and save some of it for a future date. This can be very difficult in the early addictive stages of a relationship. Nonetheless, if you set generous time limits to come off the phone (a couple of hours max) then stick to it.

"Don't accept a Saturday night date after Wednesday"

In all fairness other than in rare circumstances like unexpected opportunities this is a fair rule for her. If you want to take her out give her enough time to prepare and make any necessary arrangements in advance. She's not someone you call on short notice out of boredom, she's a woman who wants to know you have plans with her not for her.

Your next appointment is:
Date:
Time:
Please call me
if you must reshedule or cancel

"Don't see him more than once or twice a week"

In the early days of dating this makes sense.

"Stop dating him if he doesn't buy you a romantic gift for your birthday on valentines"

Valentines is an overrated, although convenient if somewhat unromantic opportunity to remind her that you care. You should try and buy her a gift on her birthday even if it's just an item with symbolic worth to the both of you.

However if you have made gifts OUTSIDE those two dates and she's willing to evaluate your relationship on the level of gifts you have given her then you should get rid of her.

"Don't tell him what to do"

Take note of whether she asks and 'suggests' things to do or is just too bossy and tells you to 'go and do this' or 'go and do that'. The word 'please' often makes a world of difference, if she's a stranger to using it then take it as a warning of what's to come.

"No more than casual kissing on the first date"

Let me make this clear. Do NOT kiss on the first date. A peck on the cheek yes, but anything more than this is a no no. Physical intimacy, even a simple kiss is the fastest way to impair your judgement and make you act stupid. If you fail to remember this rule then everything that happens next is on you.

“Let him take the lead”

Women who encourage you to take the lead are gems. They have an opinion, in fact they would probably make a better decision than you, but she gets it about our egos, we need to be men. But a word of warning, if you don’t know what you’re doing then do not be afraid to ask her opinion. There is nothing wrong in working together.

“Don’t expect a man to change or try to change or try to change him”

Sadly most women will try and change you. Be warned, they love you for who you are now, if you change too much into what they claim they want you to be then they risk getting bored. Know yourself.

“Don’t open up too fast”

Ha ha ha... seriously though, this is all about sharing emotional stuff. If the vibe is right, you both will. The problem with this is that you barely know each other and yet you are sharing your innermost secrets. Take your time, imagine how you would feel if she told all her friends details of what you have just shared with her. If you wouldn’t want them to know then don’t tell her until she’s earned that trust. Be honest and open but cautious.

"Don't date a married man"

Firstly if you're in a committed relationship, you shouldn't really be dating. If she's just a friend, then tell her so she knows up front and can help you both work on making sure no romantic business starts going on.

"Love only those who love you"

This rule remains true for both of you, forever. If she is no longer into you, then let her go for someone who is.

"Slowly involve him with your family"

Before most women will let you meet her family she has to be at least a little bit serious about you. Don't push it. If it happens too fast and it's not because she's living at home with them then try and slow things down to a pace you're comfortable with. When you first meet her and get on well together then introduce her to your friends. When after a while things are still good and you have that gut feeling (or hope) that both of you are formally an item then offer to introduce her to your family.

"The man must make the first move, you must never chase him"

No matter where you are, a train, a beach, a lecture hall, a funeral or a protest march. If you're really *attracted* to her even if you feel she's out of your league then man up, approach and talk to her.

Follow your heart if it's telling you she may be the one but be sensitive to the situation. Remember, you don't really know her to be sure you would actually like her.

Women want to be noticed, especially if they've made an effort to look beautiful. Even if the only thing you can think of saying is a simple compliment, tell her. Nothing corny, just 'hi', or 'I love your natural hair style'. If you're feeling brave you can close by saying 'it really suits you' or 'it makes you look beautiful'. If she's rude then walk away, if she smiles and invites conversation then listen and engage. What do you have to lose? Don't let the opportunity pass you by.

The Darkside

This is the stuff that I really don't recommend, truth is, if you're engaging in this stuff then you've missed the point...

DESPERATE FOR SEX?

Call an ex, see if she's single and invite her out to dinner to say sorry for hurting her, beg yourself some pity sex. However be warned, despite a short while of bliss, you may be just about to reopen a serious vexed ex scenario.

THAT DIDN'T WORK AND YOU'RE STILL DESPERATE?

(Seriously not recommended)

Remember that there are always some women up for no strings attached sex BUT you must be honest about what you want, as women often (and sometimes unintentionally) become emotionally attached afterwards.

I CAN'T FIND A WOMAN MY AGE SO WHAT ABOUT A YOUNG UN?

*(WARNING – F*CKED UP SHIT)*

Under no circumstance should you attempt to date a girl under the age of 18. Although many girls bodies start to develop from the early age of 12, they still remain children despite any physical changes.

It is very easy to detect a child by talking to her, she is prone to wearing heavy makeup, giggling often, and thinking you're cool for being interested in her! You're not cool... you're a potential paedophile. Don't do it.

THE PROBLEM WITH PORN

Don't pay for it.

Not unless you're ready to admit you enjoy watching women share their sexual exploitation on camera.

Learning Stuff

Much of what occurs in porn videos is dispassionate fantasy sex. The woman is usually totally submissive and willing to perform sexual acts that would never occur with a couple engaged in genuine love making.

Whilst it may be useful to help grasp the basics of sex, it is important to understand that if you attempt to treat a real woman in the way many of these performers are depicted you could end up committing assault, being assaulted, injured, or even, arrested. For example, engaging in oral sex is a personal decision and an act that for many is very pleasurable, but anal penetration (or buggery) by penis, fingering or licking is an act that should never be practised.

What a man and a woman do in the privacy of their bedroom is private, but be careful not to be overly influenced by dangerous fetish material designed to appeal to the cash rich perverts who finance much of the industry.

Watching Together

Some women are fine with men viewing porn, but only if they are allowed to watch it with them. This can be an erotic turn on for some or, as for many, very uncomfortable depending on how you feel about it. It is very rare that a woman who is in love with you will enjoy you expressing attraction to another woman.

Don't get addicted

With the increased availability of explicit sexual material men can become detached from the reality of genuine lovemaking which must include a woman that we not only find attractive, but also share some real emotional feelings for. The self serving nature of masturbation means many men can experience intense and more frequent ejaculation by themselves but be warned, this can also render us impotent and unable to satisfactorily engage with women on an intimate level, an act which is infinitely superior.

ERR... IS IT OK TO DATE OUTSIDE MY 'RACE'?

In theory you can date and have sex with whomever you want as long as they're of legal consenting age. But when it comes to building long lasting relationships then cultural, physical and spiritual compatibility is required for true happiness.

"Love is enough"

Sigh... If only life were so simple. Love is the foundation. TRUST and RESPECT is the key.

"I don't see colour"

It's often said that love is blind. Maybe, but society is not. It's impossible to fully connect spiritually, with a person that doesn't experience, understand or for want of a better word... 'see' the world you live in and the daily struggles you encounter due to your 'colour'.

If someone doesn't see 'colour' then that person is actively rejecting your Ancestry and culture. Are you prepared to sacrifice any part of your identity? What happens if you have children? If neither of you see 'colour in your relationship then who will accept the responsibility of teaching them about their culture, Ancestry and rich dual heritage, AS WELL AS the reality of racism still prevalent in society today?

"I never date my own kind"

Why not? Have you ever dated your own 'kind'? Do you hate your own kind? Do you hate yourself? Be careful, this person may have serious 'down low' type identity issues and subconsciously not see you as a whole individual.

"It's 'racist' to only date my 'own kind'"

Grow up. Was Nelson Mandela racist? He advocated Africans and non-Africans living together in harmony but only ever married African women. What of Martin Luther King, was he 'racist'? He advocated both 'black' and 'white' coming together but his wife was an African American. It is normal, not racist to date and marry from within your ethnic group.

CHEATING AKA HOW TO LOSE HER

(Stupid and not recommended)

Before you go down the perilous path of having two women, watch a film or a drama on the same topic with your partner and talk to find out what she thinks. If you're brave then discuss the topic of polygamy and ask her if she would ever accept the position of senior/head wife.

- ☐ Invest in two mobiles, one for her and another for your understandings.
- ☐ Never give an understanding your home number unless you really, really trust her.
- ☐ Sign all cards and gifts to your understanding with an initial.
- ☐ Keep a spare shirt at work.
- ☐ Make sure you never send your understanding any letters or long emails. For one day she'll be pissed off with you, and those items will be her ammunition to bring your whole world crumbling down.
- ☐ Sex smell lingering in house, girlfriend about to arrive, fry some food (fish) and tell her you didn't know if she's eaten.
- ☐ Only interested in married women? Look for wedding band (or give away imprint) on left hand.

- Introduce your girlfriend to a fugly friend, later explain she's having some personal drama and you're the only person she trusts to honestly support her. Use her as an alibi for some late nights during the week.
- If you have to have two women then make sure their dates are different.
- Unless they both know about each other and have willingly accepted the situation, NEVER let both women meet. Ever.
- Never try new sex moves with one that you learnt with another.
- If your clothes stink of sex and perfume, go into a late night laundry and toss it in the dryer with some food or beer for two minutes.
- Understandings must live and work at least an hour's drive away from BOTH you and your partner.
- WARNING: If your best mate is female, then never meet up with her when she's single and horny and you're really pissed off with your girlfriend. One night of passion could cost you BOTH of them. Use the phone instead.

WHAT CLUES?

No matter what she pretends, your partner is not stupid, and already suspects. Your understanding may deliberately be leaving clues as she's become interested in having a long term relationship with you!!

- Cheap lipstick on clothes.
- Scratches on back.
- Incriminating sexy messages on answer machine.
- Jewellery in your car.
- Underwear in your bed.
- Strong scent of perfume on your clothes.
- A change in your routine is a dead giveaway (working late is so tired) the key is to encourage a change in her (your girlfriends) routine, encourage her to visit an old friend or family, even help her settle an old feud.

MINI GLOSSARY

African - a person who is of African ancestry (or has an African parent), irrespective of where they are born. A biological identity linked to genealogy / a person's heritage, cannot be changed or removed by law

African Caribbean - a person who is of African ancestry & Caribbean nationality (formally West Indian)

African American - a person who is of African ancestry & American nationality (formally 'black' American)

African British - a person who is of African ancestry & British nationality (or British African)

Baby Mother – an inappropriate way to describe the mother of someone's child.

Batty – Informal term for a man engaged in intimate same sex behaviour (typically anal sex / buggery).

Bitches / Ho's - phrases used by idiots to describe women

black - old fashioned and often offensive label used to describe a person who is of African heritage

BOD - a woman with curvy / voluptuous attributes "sista had a bod on her" (phat, buff)

Booty/Butt - One of nature's gift to sistas (aka Junk n da trunk)

Brotha - the coolest man on the planet earth ;-)

Coolie - an old fashioned (offensive) term for a person with dual heritage (and some Asian looking features)

Dual heritage – A person with more than one dominant ethnic identity (e.g. She is an African with european heritage)

European – A person who is of european ancestry, irrespective of where they are born.

Fugly – F*cking ugly

Foine - a fine looking sista

Lesbian – A woman engaged in same sex behaviour. Don't believe the hype, your d*ck is NOT a magic wand that can 'convert' a lesbian friend

Nationality – A legal identity linked to where a person resides, can be changed or removed by law.

N*ggaz - phrase used by an idiot to describe other idiots

Pan Africanism – The act of loving all African people irrespective of their heritage

Sista - the finest woman on the planet earth ;-)

STFU - Shut the f*ck up

Trouble - to have sex "Did you trouble her?"

Understanding (F*ck buddy) - A woman who is cool with only being a sexual play thing. The rules are one of you calls, you meet up, have dinner, see a play or film, have sex, no contact for a fortnight.

Voo - when a woman seduces you without even physically touching you (female equivalent of woo)

West Indian - old fashioned term for a person of African Caribbean heritage

white - an old fashioned term for a person of european ancestry.

Red/Redbone/Yellow/Browning – Offensive terms to describe African people with light coloured skin

Yellow – Offensive term to describe an African with light coloured skin

ABOUT THE AUTHOR

Toyin Agbetu is a father, writer, artist-activist and Pan African community worker. He was born 13 April 1967 in Hackney, London, UK and is an African of Yoruba heritage, Ogun spirit. He was schooled at Jubilee Primary and Woodberry Down Secondary School. During 2009 he studied *Education and Community Development* under the tutorage and direction of Sis Abiola Ogunsola (Dr) and Bro Kimani Nehusi (Dr) at the University of East London. In 2010 he studied Human Rights and Constitutional Law. As a filmmaker his works include *Maafa: Truth 2007*, *Maisha: Solutions* and *The Walk*. He has participated in numerous panel debates and been interviewed for various TV, radio and film productions on community issues ranging from African history to home education.

During the 1980 - 90's he formed his own record labels, including *Unyque Artists* and *Intrigue Records* and became a prolific musician releasing numerous recordings on various major and independent labels under production pseudonyms including the Dark Knight, Master T, Nemesis, 2Tuff and Deluxe. After his father's passing in 1996, he founded the Ligali Organisation (2000) in his name, where as an educationalist and journalist he has published political, social and cultural media for African people worldwide. His international profile increased when on 23 March 2007 he successfully challenged the British monarch, church and government at Westminster Abbey, London at their public ritual of disrespect to the millions of African people lost during Maafa.

SOME OF TOYIN'S FAVOURITE BOOKS

1. The Healers/Two Thousand Season – *Ayi Kwei Armah*
2. Speaking Truth to Power – *Tajudeen Abdul Raheem*
3. Autobiography of Malcolm X – *Malik El-Shabazz*
4. Gods Bits of Wood – *Ousmane Sembene*
5. Spirit of Intimacy - *Sobonfu Somé*
6. Africans at the Crossroads: African World Revolution – *John Henrik Clarke*
7. Destruction of Black Civilisation – *Chancellor Williams*
8. Pedagogy of Freedom/Oppressed – *Paulo Freire*
9. Half of a Yellow Sun / Purple Hibiscus - *Chimamanda Ngozi Adichie*
10. Black Africa: The Economic and Cultural Basis for a Federated State – *Cheikh Anta Diop*
11. Ain't I a Woman: Black Women and Feminism – *Bell Hooks*
12. Dark Matter - *Sheree R. Thomas (Editor)*
13. The River Between - *Ngugi wa Thiong'o*
14. Myth, Literature and the African World – *Wole Soyinka*
15. Things Fall Apart – *Chinua Achebe*
16. How Europe Underdeveloped Africa – *Walter Rodney*
17. Of Water and Spirit – *Malidoma Patrice Somé*
18. Wild Seed / Mind of my Mind – *Octavia Butler*
19. Wit and Wisdom of Africa – *Patrick Ibekwe*
20. African Women and Feminism: Reflecting on the Politics of Sisterhood - *Oyeronke Oyewumi*
21. Blue Skies for Africans - *Paul Ifayomi Grant*
22. Decolonising the African Mind – *Chinweizu*
23. The Philosophy and Opinions of Marcus Garvey - *Amy Jacques Garvey (Editor)*
24. Enemies: The Clash of the Races - *Haki R. Madhubuti*

Also available:

Ukweli – A Political and Spiritual basis for Pan Africanism

"Freedom and dignity through the work of liberation"

In this intimate book of instruction, Toyin Agbetu explains why Pan Africanism is still relevant in today's world. He explains how knowledge of our ancient history and wisdoms has helped win battles in a war of enslavement that begun hundreds of years ago. If you've ever wondered about your purpose and responsibility to community, or question whether rites of passage would help our children, then come follow his journey and read his words of learning in this merging of spirit and politics.

Ukweli is the Kiswahili word for Truth

Revoetry – Poems from an African British Perspective

A collection of eclectic poems from an African British perspective touching on themes from Maafa, love and relationships to identity, politrix and healing.

The Walk - DVD

On 27 March 2007 a Pan Africanist named Toyin Agbetu challenged the British Government, Monarchy and Church as they gathered to hold a religious celebration for the Bicentenary of the Abolition of the Slave Trade Act in Westminster Abbey, England. The ritual, which made no mention of the Haitian Revolution, the Middle Passage and the African freedom fighters that ended Britain's system of transatlantic and colonial enslavement focused on the acts of parliamentarian William Wilberforce.

Toyin, who condemned the service as an insult and disgrace, halted the proceedings with words that gave a voice to the collective view of millions around the world. As Maafa truths were revealed he was demonised and misrepresented in the British media as a 'lone madman'.

Watch the restored uncensored footage of what happened that day and afterwards when the African community in Britain stood beside him - from his arrest and incarceration to the eventual dropping of all criminal charges. Their journey took them from Westminster Abbey, outside Downing Street, the National Portrait Gallery, Africa House and eventually to the belongings of their Ancestors still illegally held captive in the British Museum.

This is the story of their walk...

www.ingramcontent.com/pod-product-compliance
Ingram Content Group UK Ltd.
Pitfield, Milton Keynes, MK11 3LW, UK
UKHW021050270726
13967UKWH00012B/144

9 780954 344306